Retired

Vision Board

Clip Art Book

JUST A FRIENDLY REMINDER

This book serves as a guide and is not intended to substitute professional advice. Neither the author nor the publisher can be held responsible for any loss or damage that may arise from using or misusing the book or its contents. If you have any health concerns, it's always a good idea to consult with your physician. They're the experts who can provide the best guidance for your specific needs. Your well-being is important, so make sure to seek medical supervision for any health-related matters.

TABLE OF CONTENT

MANIFEST YOUR DREAMS

Are you ready to turn your aspirations into reality in the upcoming year?

Let's create a **vision board** that will serve as your compass, guiding you toward your dreams and goals. By regularly seeing these visual representations of your goals, you will be more motivated and inspired to work toward achieving them.

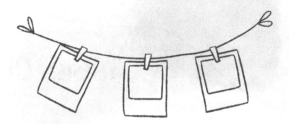

WHAT IS A VISION BOARD?

A Vision Board is a visual representation of one's **goals**, **dreams**, and **aspirations**. It typically consists of a collage of images, words, and phrases that depict what a person wants to achieve or manifest in life.

Vision boards help you clarify your goals, stay motivated, and maintain focus on your desired outcomes.

THE BENEFITS OF A VISION BOARD

- **Clarity and Focus:** It hones your focus, defining and clarifying goals to align your efforts with your desires.
- **Motivation and Inspiration:** It serves as a daily reminder of your dreams, driving motivation to act and progress toward your goals.
- **Positive Mindset:** Regular engagement with your vision board cultivates a positive mindset, replacing doubt with belief and transforming obstacles into opportunities.
- **Goal Success:** Studies suggest that vision board creators are likely to achieve their goals and dreams.
- **Visualization:** A vision board aids in visualization, helping you manifest your desires through the law of attraction.

MATERIALS

- A board (e.g., corkboard, foam board, poster board, or digital canvas).
- Scissors for cutting out images and words.
- Glue or adhesive for attaching cutouts to the board.
- Markers or colored pencils for adding personal touches and decorations.

HOW TO USE

INSTRUCTIONS

Step 1: Set Your Intentions

Be specific about your intentions and goals in various life areas, such as career, relationships, health, and personal growth.

Step 2: Gather and Cut Out

Collect images, words, and phrases from this book and other sources that represent your aspirations.

Step 3: Arrange Your Materials

Organize the materials you've collected into categories or themes based on your goals.

Step 4: Create Your Vision Board

Begin by arranging your images, words, and phrases on a board in a manner that is visually appealing and meaningful to you. Be creative and follow your intuition.

Step 5: Personalize

Add your unique touch with drawings, colors, decorations, affirmations, or personal messages.

Step 6: Visualize

Take a few moments each day to visualize your goals. Use your vision board as a source of inspiration and motivation to take action toward your aspirations.

LOOK BACK AT YOUR LIFE

1. What are some of the most valuable lessons you've learned in your life?

_____

_____

2. Remember a time that was particularly challenging and how you overcame it?

_____

_____

3. What are you most proud of achieving or accomplishing in your life?

_____

_____

4. Who were the most influential people in your life and why?

_____

_____

5. How has the world changed most significantly during your lifetime?

_____

_____

6. What advice would you give to your younger self if you could?

_____

_____

7. What were your favorite hobbies or pastimes when you were younger? Are there any you still enjoy today?

_____

_____

8. Can you share a story from your career that had a lasting impact on you?

_____

_____

9. What traditions or values do you hope to pass on to the next generations?

_____

_____

10. Looking back, what brought you the most joy and why?

_____

_____

A GENTLE REMINDER

A well-crafted vision board serves as a beacon of inspiration and motivation, reminding you of your deepest desires. Regularly revisiting your board can fuel your drive to achieve them.

However, challenges are inevitable. You might encounter frustration with slow progress or feel overwhelmed by the constant visual nudges. These emotions are perfectly normal and shared by many.

The key lies in maintaining a balanced perspective when creating your vision board. While it's a powerful tool for focus and motivation, remember that success often comes hand-in-hand with challenges. Adapting your goals and strategies along the way is a natural part of the process.

Think of your vision board as a glimpse of your future destination, but savor the journey. Embrace resilience and celebrate your progress, no matter how small.

Every End
IS A NEW
Beginning

Make
every day
Count

Live Life
to the
Fullest

NEW
Adventures
AWAIT YOU

UNSTOPPABLE

Passion Enjoy

TREASURE

Health Hope

Freedom

Moments Happy

AGE IS just a NUMBER

New chapters are exciting

Retired
but not expired

Create
and
Inspire

Blessed

Kindness

JOY

in everyday moments

Just
Breathe

NO
ALARM
CLOCK
DAYS

YOU'VE
EARNED IT!

Peace

Make It
Different

LEARN
NEW THINGS

Never too late
FOR FUN

Creativity

Time to pursue
PASSION

Let's go!

Move your body

Stay Curious
Stay Active

Celebrate
every day

If You
Never Try
You Will
Never Know

JUST DO IT

FOLLOW ♥
YOUR HEART

TRUE LOVE NEVER ENDS

Soulmate

Happy Ending

LIVE

LAUGH

LOVE

Family
is forever

Make a house
A HOME

Cherish
YOUR TRIBE

Keep family close

Family

Age gracefully, live happily

Home ~sweet~ Home

Love more, worry less

HAPPINESS
comes from
little things

L♥VE &
SUPPORT

Beloved

Content

Quality Time

In family
we trust

United

Grow old
together

My family,
my life

Friendship

Besties

Friends are Family Chosen

NEVER TOO OLD FOR
FRIENDS

Stay Pawsitive

Pets are Heart Healers

Lovely

Joy in every day

No rush, no fuss

DREAM HOUSE

Living
Life
Fully

Relaxation:
Now a priority

Enjoy
every sunset

Explore,
engage,
enjoy

Your pace,
your peace

Keep smiling

41

BALANCE

Eat more
vegetables

DRINK
MORE WATER

Sleep well

43

Self-Care

Health is
true wealth

Peaceful Mind,
Peaceful Life

Exercise

Every breath counts

NURTURE BODY, MIND, SOUL

Healthy Happy Life

Find joy in movement

Sports

Wellness

Breathe deeply

Socialize   Revitalize

Energize

New friends,
New adventures

Together   Stay vibrant

Volunteer,
make a difference

Stay connected

MASTERFUL

LEARNING
NEVER AGES

CHALLENGE
YOUR MIND

WISDOM
NEVER GETS OLD

TEACH,
LEARN,
REPEAT

BOOKS
open new worlds

Education
is timeless

Knowledge

START-UP

Endlessly valuable

Launch
NEW VENTURES

Retire from job, not work

Follow Your Bliss

Wanderlust

Freedom

Make every day
COUNT

Adventurous

Time to thrive

Every day's
a holiday

Break free

Let
THE FUN
begin

Vacation
Forever

Plant new roots

Spring again

Fuji Mount

Pyramids of Giza

Eiffel Tower

Statue of Liberty

Great Wall of China

Ha Long Bay

The Taj Mahal

Corcovado
and Cristo Redentor

Sydney Opera House

Red Square

Easter Island

The Colosseum

Stonehenge

Machu Picchu

Tibet

AAAAAABBBBBB
CCCCDDDDDEE
EEEFFFFFGG
GGGHHHHHHI
IIIIJJJJKKKK
LLLLLMMMM
MNNNNNOOOO

PPPPPQQQRR
RRRSSSSST
TTTTUUUUUV
VVVWWWXX
XXYYYYYYZ
ZZZ11122
23344455

666 7777 888

999 000 ! ! !

??? , , . " "

" " * * @ @ #

$ $ % % & & +

+ = = (( ))

Make your retirement is a JOURNEY not a DESTINATION

Made in the USA
Las Vegas, NV
23 December 2024

15300372R00046